Jumpstarters for Math

Short Daily Warm-ups for the Classroom

By
CINDY BARDEN

COPYRIGHT © 2005 Mark Twain Media, Inc.

ISBN 1-58037-297-X

Printing No. CD-404023

Mark Twain Media, Inc., Publishers
Distributed by Carson-Dellosa Publishing Company, Inc.

Table of Contents

Introduction

Physical warm-ups help athletes prepare for more strenuous types of activity. Mental warm-ups help students prepare for the day's lesson while reviewing what they have previously learned.

The short warm-up activities presented in this book provide teachers and parents with activities to help students practice the skills they have already learned. Each page contains five warm-ups—one for each day of the week. Used at the beginning of class, warm-ups help students focus on a math-related topic. A page of challenging brain teasers is included at the end of the book.

The warm-ups include addition, subtraction, multiplication, division, fractions, decimals, math stories, number sense, place value, geometry, algebra, graphing, statistics, measurement, and probability activities. They can be used in any order to best meet your teaching needs. Assume that all fractions should be reduced to lowest terms.

Suggestions for use:

- Copy and cut apart one page each week. Give students one warm-up activity each day at the beginning of class.

- Give each student a copy of the entire page to complete day by day. Students can keep the completed pages in a three-ring binder to use as a resource for review.

- Make transparencies of individual warm-ups and complete the activities as a group.

- Provide extra copies of warm-ups in your learning center for students to complete at random when they have spare time.

- Keep some warm-ups on hand to use as fill-ins when the class has a few extra minutes before lunch or dismissal.

Math Warm-ups:

Number Sense and Place Value

Name/Date _____

Number Sense and Place Value 1

Write the individual digits of the numbers below in the correct places on the place value chart.

	ten thousands	thousands	hundreds	tens	ones
A. 43,067					
B. 5,439					
C. 10,080					
D. 41,001					

Name/Date _____

Number Sense and Place Value 2

Write each number in words.

A. 31,438 _____

B. 17,091 _____

C. 3,007 _____

D. 814,737 _____

_____

E. 1,215,076 _____

_____

Name/Date _____

Number Sense and Place Value 3

A. Write a four-digit number greater than 8,351 with 6 in the tens place.

_____

B. Write a four-digit number less than 2,686 using all odd numbers.

_____

Name/Date _____

Number Sense and Place Value 4

Write the expanded form for each number.

A. 739   = _____ + _____ + _____

B. 4,078   = _____ + _____ + _____
             + _____

C. 9,190   = _____ + _____ + _____
             + _____

D. 17,376 = _____ + _____ + _____
             + _____ + _____

Name/Date _____

Number Sense and Place Value 5

Arrange each group of numbers in order from least to greatest.

A. 17,717;   77,117;   11,171;   17,117

_____ _____ _____ _____

B. 32,287;   83,872;   27,822;   27,827

_____ _____ _____ _____

C. 456,654;   654,456;   456,456;   654,654

_____ _____ _____ _____

Math Warm-ups:
Number Sense and Place Value

Name/Date _____

_____

Number Sense and Place Value 6

Compare the two numbers in each item below. Write <, >, or = in the blanks.

A. 114,441 _____ 144,114

B. 37,534 _____ 37,354

C. 71,119 _____ 71,911

D. 4,573 _____ 45,773

E. 296,864 _____ 269,864

F. 1,432,567 _____ 1,432,567

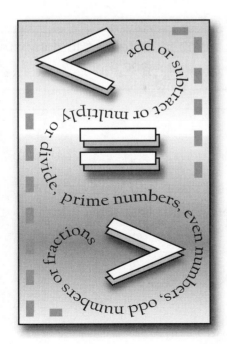

Name/Date _____

Number Sense and Place Value 7

Compare the three numbers in each item. Circle the lowest number.

A. 32,332; 23,332; 33,323
B. 42,347; 24,374; 43,437
C. 91,119; 91,991; 91,919
D. 11,110; 10,111; 11,011

LOW

Name/Date _____

Number Sense and Place Value 8

For each group of digits, write the greatest and lowest four-digit number.

A. 4, 6, 0, 6   Greatest: _____   Lowest: _____
B. 3, 1, 2, 8   Greatest: _____   Lowest: _____
C. 7, 9, 5, 7   Greatest: _____   Lowest: _____
D. 0, 9, 2, 8   Greatest: _____   Lowest: _____

Name/Date _____

Number Sense and Place Value 9

Write the numbers indicated below.

A. eighteen thousand, four hundred twenty-eight _____

B. seventy-one thousand six _____

C. 10,000 + 5,000 + 800 + 40 + 3 _____

D. 700,000 + 50,000 + 4,000 + 100 + 8 _____

Name/Date _____

Number Sense and Place Value 10

A. Write five odd numbers greater than 100.

_____

B. Write five even numbers between 37 and 73.

_____

C. Write five prime numbers greater than 5.

_____

Math Warm-ups:
Number Sense and Place Value

Name/Date _____

Number Sense and Place Value 11

A. Write a four-digit number with the digits arranged from greatest to least.

_____

B. Write the greatest possible four-digit number
using 1, 6, 5, and 0.

_____

Name/Date _____

Number Sense and Place Value 13

Compare the three numbers. Circle the greatest number.

A. 88,888; 88,088; 80,888

B. 77,373; 73,777; 73,337

C. 22,232; 32,222; 23,222

D. 11,911; 19,119; 91,991

Name/Date _____

Number Sense and Place Value 12

Arrange each group of numbers in order from
greatest to least.

A. 50,914; 41,095; 41,590; 41,905

_____   _____   _____   _____

B. 42,282; 82,842; 24,822; 24,824

_____   _____   _____   _____

C. 453,354; 354,453; 453,453; 354,354

_____   _____   _____   _____

Name/Date _____

Number Sense and Place Value 14

A. Write an equation using these digits and
symbols: 10, 3, 13, +, and =.

_____

B. Write an equation using only even numbers.

_____

C. Write two number sentences to compare
271 and 172. Use < and >.

_____

_____

Name/Date _____

Number Sense and Place Value 15

In the space below, draw a number line. Mark and label it by fives. Locate and label each of
these numbers on your number line. If you want to make a larger number line, draw it on a
sheet of paper turned horizontally.

   A. 75   B. 42   C. 57   D. 16   E. 65   F. 28

Math Warm-ups:
Addition

Name/Date _____

_____

Addition 1

A.	4	B.	11
	5		7
	6		8
	7		6
	+ 3		+ 5

C.	9	D.	3
	2		9
	13		7
	5		3
	+ 8		+ 4

E.	6	F.	6
	4		9
	2		14
	9		1
	+ 5		+ 7

Name/Date _____

Addition 2

A. 13 + 26 = _____   B. 41 + 29 = _____

C. 74 + 77 = _____   D. 85 + 48 = _____

E. 37 + 92 = _____   F. 36 + 68 = _____

Name/Date _____

Addition 3

A. Jenna had 36 CDs in her collection. Joanna had 48 CDs. How many did they have all together? _____

B. Rachel rode her horse 14 miles. Rhonda rode her camel 16 miles. How far did the two girls ride? _____

C. Joel completed 11 miles of a super-marathon relay race. Jody ran 19 miles of the race, and Jamie ran the last 13 miles. How many miles long was the race? _____

Name/Date _____

Addition 4

When it was two inches long, Laura's trumpet vine began growing five inches a day. Fill in the chart to show how long it was one week later.

Mon.	Tues.	Wed.	Thu.	Fri.	Sat.	Sun.	Mon.
2"	7"						

Name/Date _____

Addition 5

Todd took a survey. He asked people which car they liked best: Mustang, Hummer, or VW Bee- tle. He kept track using tally marks.

Mustang: ЖЖ ЖЖ ЖЖ |||| Hummer: ЖЖ ЖЖ ЖЖ ||

VW Beetle: ЖЖ ЖЖ ЖЖ ЖЖ ЖЖ ЖЖ ЖЖ |||

How many people did Todd survey? _____

Math Warm-ups:
Addition

Addition 6

Compare the equations by writing >, <, or = on the blanks.

A. 7 + 6 _____ 8 + 4

B. 7 + 8 _____ 8 + 7

C. 5 + 9 _____ 7 + 6

D. 9 + 2 _____ 8 + 3

E. 3 + 16 _____ 12 + 4

F. 11 + 9 _____ 3 + 18

Addition 7

Paco's pumpkin grew very quickly at the end of August. It weighed 38 pounds on August 30. By the next day, it weighed 40 pounds, and the day after that, it weighed 45 pounds. Each day it increased by the same amount as the day before, plus three pounds.

On another sheet of paper, draw a chart showing the daily weight of the pumpkin for 10 days starting when it weighed 38 pounds.

Addition 8

Estimate the answers by rounding the addends to the nearest 10 and then adding.

A.	B.	C.	D.	E.	F.
14	36	84	67	53	7
+ 26	+ 49	+ 77	+ 35	+ 24	+ 734

Addition 9

Complete the fact families.

A. 6 + 9 = _____

9 + _____ = 15

15 - 6 = _____

15 - _____ = 6

B. 4 + 7 = _____

_____

_____

_____

C. 8 + 7 = _____

_____

_____

_____

D. 10 + 12 = _____

_____

_____

_____

Addition 10

A. If you add two even numbers, is the sum even or odd? _____

B. If you add two odd numbers, is the sum even or odd? _____

C. If you add an even number and an odd number, is the sum even or odd? _____

D. If you add three odd numbers, is the sum even or odd? _____

Math Warm-ups:
Addition

Name/Date _____

Addition 11

Round each number to the nearest 100.

A. 357 _____   B. 546 _____

C. 295 _____   D. 749 _____

E. 611 _____   F. 403 _____

Name/Date _____

Addition 12

A. What number is 100 more than 1,172?

_____

B. What number is 1,000 more than 1,172?

_____

C. What number is 10,000 more than 1,172?

_____

D. What number is 100,000 more than 1,172?

_____

Name/Date _____

Addition 13

When rounding to the nearest 100, what are the greatest and least numbers that can be rounded to 500?

Greatest = _____

Least = _____

Name/Date _____

Addition 14

A. George Washington was born in 1732. He became the President of the United States when he was 57 years old. In what year did he become president? _____

B. Wisconsin became the thirtieth state in 1848. In what year did Wisconsin celebrate its 150th year of statehood? _____

Name/Date _____

Addition 15

Favorite Flavor	Mint	Chocolate	Vanilla	Strawberry	Caramel	Pecan	Lemon
Number	17	61	48	23	52	28	9

A. How many liked one of the top three favorite flavors best? _____

B. How many liked chocolate or vanilla best? _____

C. How many were surveyed in all? _____

D. How many liked mint, pecan, or lemon best? _____

Math Warm-ups:
Addition

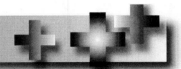

Name/Date _____

Addition 16

Complete the addition facts charts. Add the top number to each number in the left column.

A.

+	8
15	23
33	
75	
94	
47	

B.

+	11
42	
36	
54	
72	
24	

C.

+	9
49	
42	
56	
28	
77	

D.

+	12
56	
64	
24	
32	
72	

Name/Date _____

Addition 17

A. For breakfast, Tina had a medium apple containing 80 calories, two eggs containing 60 calories each, and a glass of whole milk with 165 calories. How many calories total was Tina's breakfast? _____

B. Tina's brother ate a medium banana containing 100 calories, a cup of oatmeal with 130 calories, and a cup of skim milk containing 85 calories. How many calories did her brother have in all? _____

Name/Date _____

Addition 18

Round each number to the nearest 1,000.

A. 3,257 _____

B. 1,768 _____

C. 32,047 _____

D. 81,049 _____

Name/Date _____

Addition 19

When rounding to the nearest 1,000, what are the greatest and least numbers that can be rounded to 10,000?

Greatest = _____

Least = _____

10,000

Name/Date _____

Addition 20

A. Alaska and Hawaii became the 49th and 50th states in 1959. In what year will these two states celebrate their 150th anniversary of statehood? _____

B. Columbus first sailed to the New World in 1492. How many years ago was that?

_____

Math Warm-ups:
Subtraction

Name/Date _____

Subtraction 1

A. 17 - 4 = _____   B. 25 - 8 = _____

C. 13 - 8 = _____   D. 42 - 6 = _____

E. 39 - 13 = _____   F. 40 - 12 = _____

40-17=?   ?-9=5   16-11=?

Name/Date _____

Subtraction 2

A. Jenna has 36 CDs in her collection. Jo-anna has 48 CDs. How many more CDs does Joanna have? _____

B. Rosella had 74 pairs of shoes. Cora had 25 pairs of shoes. How many more pairs of shoes did Rosella have? _____

Name/Date _____

Subtraction 3

Lyle went on a diet when he weighed 372 pounds.

Week	1	2	3	4	5	6	7	8
Pounds Lost	3	8	13	4	1	0	9	4

How much did he weigh after eight weeks on his diet? _____

Name/Date _____

Subtraction 4

A. If you subtract an even number from a different even number, is the answer odd or even? _____

B. If you subtract an even number from an odd number, is the answer odd or even? _____

C. If you subtract an odd number from an even number, is the answer odd or even? _____

D. If you subtract an odd number from a different odd number, is the answer odd or even? _____

Name/Date _____

Subtraction 5

A. What number is 100 less than 101,172? _____

B. What number is 1,000 less than 101,172? _____

C. What number is 10,000 less than 101,172? _____

D. What number is 100,000 less than 101,172? _____

9

Math Warm-ups:
Subtraction

Name/Date _____

Subtraction 6

Compare the equations by writing >, <, or = on the blanks.

A. 17 - 6 _____ 21 - 10   B. 27 - 18 _____ 18 - 7

C. 35 - 9 _____ 37 - 6   D. 19 - 12 _____ 18 - 13

E. 53 - 16 _____ 42 - 4   F. 111 - 12 _____ 113 - 18

Name/Date _____

Subtraction 7

Complete the number patterns.

A. 0   -3   -6   _____   _____   _____

B. 71   67   63   _____   _____   _____

C. 99   _____ 77   _____   _____   _____

D. 711 610 509   _____   _____   _____

Name/Date _____

Subtraction 8

A. 21 - _____ = 9   B. 43 - _____ = 19

C. 18 - _____ = 7   D. 71 - _____ = 37

E. 28 - _____ = 17   F. 26 - _____ = 17

Name/Date _____

Subtraction 9

A. In 1800, Thomas Jefferson was elected president at the age of 57. In what year was he born? _____

B. Ronald Reagan was elected president in 1980 when he was 69 years old. In what year was he born?

_____

Name/Date _____
_____

Subtraction 10

A.   214
   -   26

B.   336
   -   49

C.   84
   -   77

D.   67
   -   35

E.   53
   -   24

F.   827
   - 734

Math Warm-ups:
Subtraction

Name/Date _____

Subtraction 11
Round numbers to the nearest 10, and then subtract.

A. 341
   - 39

B. 215
   - 45

C. 608
   - 68

D. 481
   - 23

Name/Date _____

Subtraction 12
Start in the outer ring of each circle. Then fill in the numbers in the middle ring that result in the difference shown in the inner ring.

A.
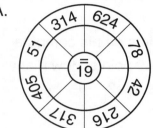

B.
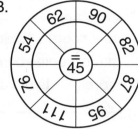

Name/Date _____

Subtraction 13
A. Coach Clark had $357.56 in his department checking account.
    He spent $23.85 for tennis balls. How much did he have left? _____

B. Next, Coach Clark wrote a check for $65 to have the snow shoveled from the tennis court.
    How much was left in his account? _____

C. Coach Clark sent a check to a company for $79.38 to purchase a new net. What was the
    balance in his checkbook after writing the third check? _____

D. Coach Clark wanted to ask for additional money for his department. How much did he
    need to raise the amount in his account to $500? _____

Name/Date _____

Subtraction 14
A. Abby paid for a CD with a $20 bill. She received $3.17 in change. How much did the CD cost? _____

B. Josh bought a new football jersey on sale for $57.82. He used cash and a $25 gift card. How much cash did he need?

_____

Name/Date _____

Subtraction 15
Circle "T" for true or "F" for false.

A. T F The order in which numbers are subtracted does not matter.

B. T F The answer in a subtraction equation is called the product.

C. T F All negative numbers are less than zero.

D. T F Negative numbers can be subtracted but not added.

Math Warm-ups:
Subtraction

Subtraction 16

A. Rachel rode her motorcycle 341 miles. Rhonda rode her camel 162 miles. How much farther did Rachel ride?

_____

B. Joel scored 1,725 points on his computer game. Jodie scored 389 points. How many more points did Joel score?

_____

Subtraction 17

Round numbers to the nearest 100, and then subtract.

A.   468
   - 339

B.   914
   - 194

C.   349
   - 151

D.   253
   - 78

Subtraction 18

A. Tim spent 79¢ for a soda and $1.25 for a slice of pie. How much change did he receive from a five-dollar bill? _____

B. Jeremy spent $47.83 at the sports store. He only had $18.94 in cash, so he put the rest on his charge card. How much did he charge? _____

Subtraction 19

A. Missouri celebrated its 150th year of statehood in 1971. In what year did Missouri become a state? _____

B. Jay's great-great grandpa celebrated his 103rd birthday in 2001. In what year was he born? _____

Subtraction 20

Draw a number line for each equation on another sheet of paper. Show the equation on the number line like the example given below for the equation: 30 - 7 = 23.

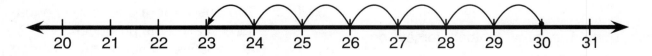

A. 15 - 7 = _____   B. 82 - 5 = _____   C. 47 - 19 = _____

Math Warm-ups: Multiplication

Name/Date _____

Multiplication 1

A. 4 x 6 = _____   B. 7 x 8 = _____

C. 9 x 6 = _____   D. 7 x 5 = _____

E. 8 x 8 = _____   F. 6 x 11 = _____

Name/Date _____

Multiplication 2

A. How many? _____   B. How many? _____

```
********
********
********
********
```

@ @ @ @ @
@ @ @ @ @
@ @ @ @ @
@ @ @ @ @

C. How many? _____

```
&&&&&&&&&&
&&&&&&&&&&
&&&&&&&&&&
```

Name/Date _____

Multiplication 3

Compare the equations. Write >, <, or = on the blanks.

A. 3 x 4 _____ 6 x 4   B. 3 x 14 _____ 12 x 4

C. 7 x 7 _____ 5 x 9   D. 11 x 4 _____ 9 x 6

E. 4 x 12 _____ 6 x 8   F. 10 x 7 _____ 4 x 14

Name/Date _____

Multiplication 4

A. Jerry, Terry, and Merry each have $17. How much do they have all together? _____
B. Harry, Larry, and Kerry each jogged 36 miles last week. How many miles all together? _____
C. Holly, Dolly, and Polly each picked 84 quarts of strawberries. How many quarts all together? _____

Name/Date _____
_____

Multiplication 5

A. 3 monkeys: each has 4 bananas. How many bananas? _____

B. 7 pigs: each pig wears 3 pink bows. How many bows? _____

C. 4 baby giraffes: each giraffe has 28 spots. How many spots? _____

D. 9 cases of widgets: each case weighs 125 pounds. How many pounds in all? _____

E. 9 cases of widgets: each case contains 200 widgets. How many widgets? _____

Math Warm-ups:
Multiplication

Name/Date _____

Multiplication 6

A.　21
　　x 5

B.　36
　　x 3

C.　41
　　x 6

D.　70
　　x 8

E.　57
　　x 7

F.　98
　　x 4

```
 66
 x8
528

19.00
  x4
76.00

 126
 X31
3906
```

Name/Date _____

Multiplication 7

A. 7 toddlers: 32 toys each. How many toys all together? _____

B. 11 leopards: 79 spots each. How many spots in all? _____

C. 9 boxes of disks: 35 disks in each box. How many disks in all? _____

D. 8 helpings of real mashed potatoes. 14 lumps in each helping. How many lumps in all? _____

Name/Date _____

Multiplication 8

Commutative property of numbers: The order in which numbers are multiplied does not affect the product.

Write four examples that show the commutative property of multiplication.

_____　　_____

_____　　_____

Name/Date _____

Multiplication 9

Write the missing factors in the middle ring. The product is on the outside ring.

A.
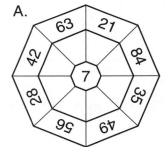

B.
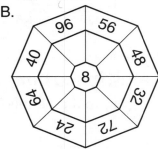

Name/Date _____

Multiplication 10

Rob's Rental Rates

circus tent	$73/day	juggler	$19/hour	lion tamer	$73/hour
clown	$27/hour	lion	$114/hour	elephant	$125/hour

A. How much would it cost to rent a juggler for three hours? _____

B. How much would it cost to rent a circus tent for four days? _____

C. How much would it cost to rent a clown for six hours? _____

D. How much would it cost to rent a lion tamer and three lions for two hours? _____

Math Warm-ups: Multiplication

Name/Date _____

_____

Multiplication 11

Crystal Cave had 186 visitors an hour for six hours on Monday. Admission is $5.00 per adult and $3.00 per child. Half the visitors on Monday were adults and half were children.

A. How many visitors went to Crystal Cave on Monday?

_____

B. How much did Crystal Cave earn in adult admission fees on Monday?

_____

C. How much in child admission fees?

_____

D. Each visitor spent an average of $4.00 in the cafeteria on Monday. How much did visitors spend in the cafeteria?

_____

Name/Date _____

Multiplication 12

A. 14	B. 46	C. 72	D. 44
x 41	x 64	x 27	x 44

Name/Date _____

Multiplication 13

On another sheet of paper, draw an array for each multiplication equation. Fill in the answers below.

A. 7 x 6 = _____   B. 9 x 5 = _____

C. 11 x 11 = _____   D. 13 x 4 = _____

Name/Date _____

Multiplication 14

A. Jessie bought five packages of radish seeds at 23¢ each. How much did she spend on radish seeds? _____

B. Jessie bought four yellow rose bushes for $3.99 each. How much did she spend on rose bushes? _____

C. Jessie ordered eight tons of pea gravel at $17.23 per ton. How much did Jessie spend on pea gravel? _____

Name/Date _____

Multiplication 15

A. Lisa has three quarters, five dimes, seven nickels, and 12 pennies. How much does she have in all? _____

B. Jim has five quarters, 12 dimes, four nickels, and 28 pennies. How much does he have all together? _____

C. Josh has two half dollars, 12 quarters, four dimes, and 16 nickels. How much money does Josh have? _____

Math Warm-ups:
Division

Name/Date _____

Division 1

A. 81 ÷ 9 = _____   B. 63 ÷ 7 = _____

C. 56 ÷ 7 = _____   D. 42 ÷ 6 = _____

E. 48 ÷ 12 = _____   F. 54 ÷ 9 = _____

Name/Date _____

Division 2

A. 83 ÷ 8 = _____R_____

B. 17 ÷ 4 = _____R_____

C. 36 ÷ 9 = _____R_____

D. 78 ÷ 6 = _____R_____

E. 57 ÷ 3 = _____R_____

F. 68 ÷ 5 = _____R_____

Name/Date _____

Division 3

A. 48 mice divided into 4 equal groups. How many in each group?
_____

B. 384 widgets packed into 8 cases. How many in each case? _____

C. 621 chocolate stars packed into 9 bags. How many in each bag? _____

D. 238 pounds of cheese cut into 8-ounce blocks. How many blocks of cheese?
_____

Name/Date _____

Division 4

A. Jenny read 22 pages of a novel each day. How many days did it take her to finish a 264-page novel? _____

B. Brenda blew up 17 helium balloons in 35 minutes. How many balloons did she blow up in an hour and 45 minutes? _____

C. Carlos took 126 photos while on vacation. He arranged the photos in an album with six photos per page. How many pages did he fill with his vacation photos? _____

Name/Date _____

Division 5

Complete the division facts charts. Divide each number in the left column by the number at the top of the chart.

A.

÷	5
15	3
35	
75	
90	
30	

B.

÷	6
42	
36	
54	
72	
24	

C.

÷	7
49	
42	
56	
28	
77	

D.

÷	8
56	
64	
24	
32	
72	

Math Warm-ups:
Division

Name/Date _____

Division 6
Complete the chart.

A. 9 x _____ = 63
    63 ÷ 9 = _____
    _____ x 9 = 63
    63 ÷ _____ = 9

B. 8 x _____ = 56
    56 ÷ 8 = _____
    _____ x 8 = 56
    56 ÷ _____ = 8

C. 7 x _____ = 42
    42 ÷ 7 = _____
    _____ x 7 = 42
    42 ÷ _____ = 7

Name/Date _____

Division 7
Double-check your answers by multiplying.

A. $6\overline{)528}$
      x 6

B. $7\overline{)455}$
      x 7

Name/Date _____

Division 8
Complete these on your own paper.
A. Write a division equation that has a quotient of 174 and a remainder of 2.
B. Write a division equation that has a quotient of 67 and a remainder of 7.
C. Write a division equation that has a divisor of 18 and no remainder.

Name/Date _____

Division 9

A. 83 ÷ 7 = _____ R _____

B. 99 ÷ 8 = _____ R _____

C. 36 ÷ 11 = _____ R _____

D. 76 ÷ 3 = _____ R _____

E. 51 ÷ 6 = _____ R _____

F. 54 ÷ 5 = _____ R _____

Name/Date _____

_____

Division 10

List eight ways to divide 80 objects with an even number of objects in each group. For example, one way would be 10 groups with 8 objects in each group.

A. _____ groups with _____ in each group

B. _____ groups with _____ in each group

C. _____ groups with _____ in each group

D. _____ groups with _____ in each group

E. _____ groups with _____ in each group

F. _____ groups with _____ in each group

G. _____ groups with _____ in each group

H. _____ groups with _____ in each group

Math Warm-ups:
Division

Name/Date _____

_____

Division 11

A. Ha Ha Cereal

Serving Size = 4 ounces

Box contains 48 ounces

How many servings?

_____

B. Hee Hee Instant Tea

Serving Size = 6 ounces

Jar makes 78 ounces

How many servings?

_____

C. Ho Ho Popcorn

Serving Size = 8 ounces

Tub contains 96 ounces

How many servings?

_____

Name/Date _____

Division 12

A. Jacob drove 468 miles in 9 hours. On the average, how many miles did he drive per hour? _____

B. Six cafeteria workers dished out 645 bowls of mustard and chocolate chip soup. On the average, how many bowls did each worker dish out? _____

Name/Date _____

Division 13

A. The school librarian kept track of the number of students using the Internet each day for a week:

Mon.: 57   Tues.: 39   Wed.: 76   Thu.: 87   Fri.: 91

On the average, how many students used the Internet each day? _____

Name/Date _____

Division 14

A. Spencer bought four 12-packs of soda for his party. Each person at the party drank two sodas. There were 22 sodas left. How many people were at the party? _____

B. Maria made 72 tacos for her friends and family. Each person ate six tacos, and they were all gone. How many people ate tacos? _____

Name/Date _____

Division 15

Rosa made up eight bouquets of flowers for her friends with the same number of each type of flower. She used the leftover flowers to make a bouquet for herself. She had 19 irises, 28 daisies, 35 carnations, and 15 lilies. How many of each type were in the bouquets?

	Irises	Daisies	Carnations	Lilies
Friends' bouquets:	____	____	____	____
Rosa's bouquet:	____	____	____	____

Math Warm-ups:

Multi-Step Equations

Name/Date _____

Multi-Step Equations 1

A. 7 + 6 + 3 - 6 - 3 + 2 - 8 = _____

B. 4 - 3 + 6 + 7 - 4 - 7 + 3 + 8 = _____

C. 9 - 9 + 8 - 7 + 6 - 5 + 4 - 3 + 3 - 2 = _____

Name/Date _____

Multi-Step Equations 2

A. Emilio worked for 6 hours and earned $5 an hour at one part-time job. He earned a total of $24 at another job that paid $6 an hour. How many hours did Emilio work all together? _____

B. How much did Emilio earn all together? _____

Name/Date _____

Multi-Step Equations 3

A. Ellen bought three items: a computer program for $29.73, copy paper for $4.97, and a package of blank CDs for $5.86. How much change did she get from a $50 bill?

_____

B. Ben's bill at the grocery store came to $47.92. He used three coupons for 40¢, 75¢, and 50¢ off. What was Ben's final cost? _____

Name/Date _____

Multi-Step Equations 4

Fill in the blanks with <, >, or =.

A. 27 ÷ 3 _____ 3 x 3

B. 2 x 7 _____ 49 ÷ 7

C. 87 - 9 _____ 72 + 19

D. 64 + 18 _____ 9 x 9

Name/Date _____

Multi-Step Equations 5

A. Which is the better buy: two 12-ounce cans of tuna for $1.49 or one 8-ounce can for 79¢? _____

B. Which is the best buy: 6 pairs of socks for $6.99, 3 pairs for $3.99, or one pair for $1.13? _____

Math Warm-ups:

Fractions

Name/Date _____

Fractions 1

Color the correct number of seashells in each group to represent $\frac{2}{3}$.

A.

B.

Name/Date _____

Fractions 2

Simplify.

A. $\frac{4}{16}$ = _____   B. $\frac{8}{12}$ = _____

C. $\frac{3}{15}$ = _____   D. $\frac{12}{36}$ = _____

E. $\frac{6}{10}$ = _____   F. $\frac{14}{16}$ = _____

Name/Date _____

Fractions 3

Write the fractions in order from least to greatest.

A. $\frac{1}{2}$ $\frac{3}{4}$ $\frac{7}{8}$ $\frac{5}{8}$ $\frac{7}{10}$ _____

B. $\frac{3}{9}$ $\frac{7}{8}$ $\frac{6}{9}$ $\frac{2}{5}$ $\frac{8}{10}$ _____

C. $\frac{8}{1}$ $\frac{1}{8}$ $\frac{7}{8}$ $\frac{7}{1}$ $\frac{1}{7}$ _____

Name/Date _____

Fractions 4

Rewrite these improper fractions as mixed numbers.

A. $\frac{37}{11}$ _____   B. $\frac{14}{8}$ _____

C. $\frac{81}{9}$ _____   D. $\frac{138}{3}$ _____

Name/Date _____

_____

Fractions 5

Write the fractions to represent the shaded part of each shape.

A. _____

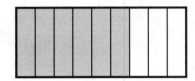

B. _____

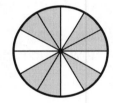

C. _____

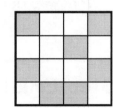

D. _____

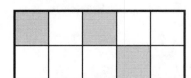

Math Warm-ups:

Fractions

Name/Date _____

Fractions 6

A.

What fraction of the arrows point left? _____

B.

What fraction of the balls are footballs? _____

C.

What fraction of the faces are not happy? _____

Name/Date _____

Fractions 7

Draw pictures on another sheet of paper to show these fractions.

A. Round pie cut into eighths: $\frac{1}{2}$ red

B. Square pan of brownies cut into sixteenths: $\frac{1}{4}$ blue

C. Round pizza cut into sixths: $\frac{1}{3}$ with pepperoni

D. Square cake cut into ninths: $\frac{2}{3}$ with green frosting

---

Name/Date _____

Fractions 8

Add.

A. $\frac{3}{4} + \frac{2}{4} =$ _____

B. $\frac{3}{7} + \frac{5}{7} =$ _____

C. $\frac{7}{9} + \frac{4}{9} =$ _____

D. $\frac{5}{8} + \frac{7}{8} =$ _____

E. $\frac{2}{6} + \frac{5}{6} =$ _____

F. $\frac{11}{12} + \frac{11}{12} =$ _____

Name/Date _____

Fractions 9

Draw pictures on another sheet of paper to show these fractions.

A. 36 cherries: $\frac{2}{3}$ red

B. 42 stars: $\frac{1}{7}$ blue

C. 25 marbles: $\frac{1}{5}$ yellow

D. 28 leaves: $\frac{3}{7}$ green

Name/Date _____

Fractions 10

Subtract.

A. $\frac{7}{8} - \frac{2}{8} =$ _____

B. $\frac{5}{9} - \frac{3}{9} =$ _____

C. $\frac{4}{6} - \frac{1}{2} =$ _____

D. $\frac{1}{2} - \frac{3}{8} =$ _____

E. $\frac{8}{10} - \frac{1}{2} =$ _____

F. $4 - \frac{2}{3} =$ _____

Math Warm-ups:

Fractions

Name/Date _____

Fractions 11

A. Twelve people in a group said broccoli was their favorite vegetable. If $\frac{2}{3}$ of the group preferred broccoli, how many were in the group? _____

B. The baseball team has 27 players. Nine are girls. What fraction of the team are girls? _____

C. Of 125 cars in a parking lot, $\frac{1}{5}$ were red. How many were red? _____

Name/Date _____

Fractions 12

Write the lowest common denominator for each pair of fractions.

A. $\frac{2}{3}$ and $\frac{3}{9}$ ____   B. $\frac{1}{5}$ and $\frac{7}{16}$ ____

C. $\frac{3}{8}$ and $\frac{3}{12}$ ____   D. $\frac{1}{2}$ and $\frac{12}{25}$ ____

E. $\frac{1}{6}$ and $\frac{1}{16}$ ____

F. $\frac{3}{36}$ and $\frac{1}{12}$ ____

Name/Date _____

Fractions 13

Change these fractions to decimals.

A. $\frac{3}{10}$ ____   B. $\frac{5}{8}$ ____

C. $\frac{6}{24}$ ____   D. $\frac{4}{32}$ ____

E. $\frac{7}{8}$ ____   F. $\frac{7}{28}$ ____

G. $\frac{6}{16}$ ____   H. $\frac{90}{100}$ ____

Name/Date _____

Fractions 14

Draw pictures on another sheet of paper showing parts of a group to represent each fraction.

A. $\frac{1}{12}$ shaded   B. $\frac{3}{5}$ white

C. $\frac{5}{6}$ dotted   D. $\frac{7}{12}$ striped

Name/Date _____

Fractions 15

A. Color $\frac{2}{5}$ of the stars blue.

Color $\frac{6}{15}$ of the stars red.
How many stars remain white? _____

☆☆☆☆☆☆☆☆☆☆☆☆
☆☆☆☆☆☆☆☆☆☆☆☆☆
☆☆☆☆☆☆☆☆☆☆☆☆☆

B. Color $\frac{1}{3}$ of the pentagons green.

Color $\frac{1}{4}$ of the pentagons brown.

Color $\frac{1}{6}$ of the pentagons red.

Leave $\frac{3}{12}$ of the pentagons white.

⬠⬠⬠⬠⬠⬠⬠⬠⬠⬠⬠⬠
⬠⬠⬠⬠⬠⬠⬠⬠⬠⬠⬠⬠
⬠⬠⬠⬠⬠⬠⬠⬠⬠⬠⬠⬠
⬠⬠⬠⬠⬠⬠⬠⬠⬠⬠⬠⬠

Math Warm-ups:
Fractions

Name/Date _____

Fractions 16

Multiply the fraction in the center by the numbers around it. Write the answers in the outer part of the ring.

A.

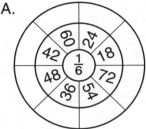

B.

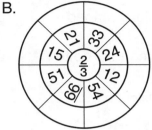

Name/Date _____

Fractions 17

Convert these fractions to percents.

A. $\frac{1}{2}$ _____

B. $\frac{3}{4}$ _____

C. $\frac{7}{10}$ _____

D. $\frac{65}{100}$ _____

E. $\frac{4}{100}$ _____

F. $\frac{1}{4}$ _____

Name/Date _____

Fractions 18

A. $\frac{2}{3} \times \frac{1}{3} =$ _____   B. $\frac{1}{4} \times \frac{3}{7} =$ _____

C. $\frac{2}{9} \times \frac{5}{8} =$ _____   D. $\frac{1}{12} \times \frac{1}{4} =$ _____

E. $\frac{2}{16} \times \frac{1}{9} =$ _____   F. $\frac{3}{8} \times \frac{5}{7} =$ _____

Name/Date _____

Fractions 19

A. Adam has 6 coins: $\frac{1}{2}$ are dimes, $\frac{2}{6}$ are pennies, and the rest are nickels. How much does Adam have? _____

B. Angie has 8 coins: $\frac{1}{2}$ are quarters, $\frac{1}{4}$ are dimes, $\frac{1}{8}$ are nickels, and the rest are pennies. How much does she have? _____

Name/Date _____

Fractions 20

A. $\frac{1}{7} \div \frac{3}{7} =$ _____

B. $\frac{3}{9} \div \frac{2}{9} =$ _____

C. $\frac{4}{5} \div \frac{2}{5} =$ _____

D. $\frac{1}{8} \div 7 =$ _____

Math Warm-ups:

Fractions

Name/Date _____

_____

Fractions 21

A. Write a math story that uses fractions.

_____

_____

_____

_____

_____

_____

_____

_____

_____

_____

_____

_____

_____

_____

B. Trade with a partner, solve your partner's question, and then check the answers.

Partner's answer to the story problem above:

_____

_____

_____

_____

_____

Name/Date _____

Fractions 22

Draw pictures on another sheet of paper to show each fraction.

A. circle: $\frac{3}{7}$ striped   B. rectangle: $\frac{2}{9}$ white

C. diamond: $\frac{3}{8}$ dotted   D. square: $\frac{2}{5}$ shaded

---

Name/Date _____

Fractions 23

Write the next three fractions to continue the pattern.

A. $\frac{1}{2}$ $\frac{1}{4}$ $\frac{1}{8}$ ____   ____   ____

B. $\frac{2}{16}$ $\frac{4}{16}$ $\frac{6}{16}$ ____   ____   ____

C. $\frac{11}{12}$ $\frac{9}{12}$ $\frac{7}{12}$ ____   ____   ____

Name/Date _____

Fractions 24

Cassie has two half dollars, four quarters, ten dimes, 20 nickels, and eight pennies.

A. What fraction of her coins are nickels? _____

B. What fraction of her coins are pennies? _____

C. What fraction of her coins are not pennies? _____

Name/Date _____

Fractions 25

A. What fraction of the students in your classroom today are girls? _____

B. What fraction of the students in your classroom today are wearing red or pink?

_____

Math Warm-ups:

Math Terms to Know

Math Terms to Know 1

Fill in the blanks with the words below.

**denominator difference dividend
divisor   numerator**

A. The answer in a subtraction equation: _____

B. The bottom number of a fraction: _____

C. The top number of a fraction: _____

D. A number divided by another number: _____

E. A number that divides another number:

_____

Math Terms to Know 2

Match.

    a. addend   b. factor   c. product
    d. quotient e. subtrahend   f. sum

A. ____ A number subtracted from another number

B. ____ Answer to a multiplication equation

C. ____ Answer to an addition equation

D. ____ A number multiplied by another number

E. ____ Answer to a division equation

F. ____ One of two or more numbers added together

Math Terms to Know 3

Circle "T" for true or "F" for false.

A. T F An improper fraction is a number whose numerator is greater than or equal to its denominator.

B. T F An improper fraction is a number whose denominator is greater than or equal to its numerator.

C. T F < is a symbol that means less than.

D. T F A lowercase x is sometimes used as a symbol for division.

E. T F Third, fifth, and seventh are examples of ordinal numbers.

Math Terms to Know 4

A. Circle the quotient: $8 \div 4 = 2$

B. Circle the product: $4 \times 8 = 32$

C. Circle the sum: $4 + 8 = 12$

D. Circle the difference: $8 - 2 = 6$

E. Circle the denominator: $\frac{4}{8}$

Math Terms to Know 5

Circle the answers.

A. A mixed number: $3\frac{1}{2}$ 3.5   350%

B. Equivalent fractions: $\frac{1}{2}$ and $\frac{4}{8}$ $\frac{1}{3}$ and $\frac{6}{9}$ $\frac{4}{9}$ and $\frac{8}{16}$

C. A prime number: 9   11   15

D. Kilogram: 10 grams   100 grams   1,000 grams

E. Equation with a remainder: $7 \div 5$ $\frac{35}{5}$ $35 \div 7$

Math Warm-ups:
Algebra

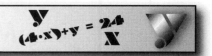

Name/Date _____

Algebra 1

Find the value of the variables.

A. $n = 6$
$n + n + n = f$
$f =$ _____

B. $p = 8$
$3 \cdot p = t$
$t =$ _____

C. $d = 8$
$d + d = e + d$
$e =$ _____

D. $g = 6$
$g + g + g = h - g$
$h =$ _____

E. $e = 7$
$42 \div e = f$
$f =$ _____

F. $j = 12$
$(j \div 3) + j = 20 - k$
$k =$ _____

Name/Date _____

Algebra 2

Fill in the missing numbers.

A. $17 +$ _____ $= 42$

B. $6 \cdot$ _____ $= 24$

C. $71 -$ _____ $= 38$

D. $72 \div$ _____ $= 8$

E. $5 + 6 +$ _____ $= 15$

F. $(3 \cdot$ _____ $) +$ _____ $= 12$

Name/Date _____

Algebra 3

Solve for y.

A. $17 + y = 42$
$y =$ _____

B. $6 \cdot y = 24$
$y =$ _____

C. $71 - y = 38$
$y =$ _____

D. $72 \div y = 8$
$y =$ _____

E. $5 + 6 + y = 15$
$y =$ _____

F. $(3 \cdot y) + y = 12$
$y =$ _____

Name/Date _____

Algebra 4

A. Calvin has 71 daisy plants. He gave many of them to his friends and had 38 left. Write and solve an equation with a variable to show how many plants he gave away.

_____

B. Velma planted 72 onions in eight rows. Write and solve an equation with a variable to show how many onions were in each row.

_____

Name/Date _____

Algebra 5

A. Melvin has 42 rose bushes. Seventeen are red, and the rest are blue. Write and solve an equation with a variable to show how many are blue.

_____

B. Alvin put 24 roses in vases, with 6 roses in each vase. Write and solve an equation with a variable to show how many vases he filled.

_____

Math Warm-ups:
Tables and Graphs

Name/Date _____

Tables and Graphs 1

Use the information from the table to make a bar graph on another sheet of paper.

Favorite Kinds of Beans					
Baked	7	Butter	11	Green	10
Jelly	16	Kidney	12	Lima	11
Pinto	8	Refried	13	Yellow	12

Name/Date _____

Tables and Graphs 2

Use the information from the Favorite Kinds of Beans table to answer the questions.

A. How many people were surveyed? _____

B. What percent liked lima beans best? _____

C. What fraction liked jelly beans best? _____

D. Write a decimal to represent those who like refried beans best. _____

Name/Date _____

Tables and Graphs 3

Use the information from the graph below to complete a table on another sheet of paper.

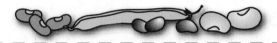

Favorite Type of Wildcat

cheetah

cougar

leopard

lion

lynx

tiger

0   5   10   15   20   25   30

Name/Date _____

Tables and Graphs 4

Use the information from the Favorite Types of Wildcat graph to answer the questions on another sheet of paper.

A. Which type of cat did most people like least?
B. Which type of cat was chosen by 50% more people than lions?
C. Write the types of cats in order from most favorite to least favorite.

Name/Date _____

Tables and Graphs 5

Use the information from the table to make a line graph on another sheet of paper.

Favorite Zoo Animals					
Bear	75	Elephant	63	Giraffe	84
Gorilla	107	Lion	98	Seal	71

Math Warm-ups:
Decimals

Name/Date _____

_____

Decimals 1

Write the equivalent decimals.

A. eight hundredths

_____

B. eleven and twelve

hundredths

_____

C. eighty-one hundredths

_____

D. fourteen and six tenths

_____

E. twenty-one hundredths

_____

F. seven and seven

hundredths

_____

Name/Date _____

Decimals 2

Rewrite the amounts using dollar signs and decimal points.

A. 456¢ _____   B. 72¢ _____

C. 1548¢ _____   D. 902¢ _____

Name/Date _____

Decimals 3

Write the decimals as fractions. Reduce to lowest terms.

A. 0.78 _____   B. 0.625 _____

C. 0.99 _____   D. 0.26 _____

Name/Date _____

Decimals 4

A. 3.7 + 4.9 = _____   B. 2.9 + 11.4 = _____

C. 7.3 + 4.7 = _____   D. 11.4 - 9.5 = _____

E. 17.2 - 8.3 = _____   F. 21 - 19.4 = _____

Name/Date _____

Decimals 5
Complete the temperature chart.

	Noon	Midnight	Difference
A.	98.7°	78.5°	_____
B.	84.5°	59.8°	_____
C.	71.3°	67.5°	_____
D.	78°	67.5°	_____

Math Warm-ups:
Decimals

Name/Date _____

Decimals 6

A. 3.7 x 4.9 = _____

B. 2.9 x 11.4 = _____

C. 7.3 x 4.7 = _____

Name/Date _____

Decimals 7

A. Melissa jogged 3.7 miles a day for 7 days. How far did she jog in all? _____

B. The Hungry Lion Cafe served 9.5 pies a day for 30 days. How many pies did they serve in all?

_____

Name/Date _____

Decimals 8

A. Toby used 8.7 gallons of gas to drive 478 miles. How many miles per gallon did he get? Round your answer to the nearest tenth. _____

B. Tony spent $23.70 on ice cream bars in June. Ice cream bars cost 79¢ each. How many did he buy?

_____

Name/Date _____

Decimals 9

Write the percents as decimals.

A. 37% = _____   B. 42% = _____

C. 91.4% = _____   D. 3.7% = _____

E. 26.5% = _____   F. 6.2% = _____

Name/Date _____

_____

Decimals 10

Shade in the appropriate number of squares on each grid to show the decimals indicated.

A. 0.75

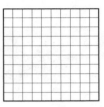

B. 0.33

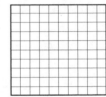

C. 0.87

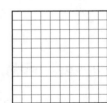

D. 0.04

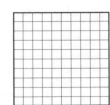

Math Warm-ups:
Decimals

Name/Date _____

Decimals 11

Write the equivalent fractions. Reduce fractions to lowest terms.

A. 3.7 = _____   B. 4.62 = _____

C. 11.1 = _____   D. 9.65 = _____

Name/Date _____

Decimals 12

A. The average customer buys 16.8 gallons of gas. If the station averages 31 customers an hour, how many gallons of gas will they sell in four hours? _____

B. Sandy, Randy, and Mandy shared the cost of a computer game that cost $31.38. How much did it cost each of them? _____

Name/Date _____

Decimals 13

Solve. Round quotients to the nearest hundredth if necessary.

A. 16.92 ÷ 4.7 = _____

B. 22.68 ÷ 6.3 = _____

C. 104.78 ÷ 12.2 = _____

D. 1,735.26 ÷ 99.07 = _____

Name/Date _____

Decimals 14

A. Ponce spent $35 for office supplies plus 5% sales tax. How much did he spend in all? _____

B. Sally spent $47 for party decorations. After adding 5% sales tax, what was her total? _____

Name/Date _____

Decimals 15

Complete the equivalency chart.

	Fraction	Percent	Decimal
A.	$\frac{7}{8}$		
B.		75%	
C.			0.725
D.		135%	
E.			0.675
F.	$\frac{4}{6}$		

Math Warm-ups:
Money

Money 1

Write the total for each group of coins.

A. 25¢ 10¢ 10¢ 1¢ 25¢ 1¢ 10¢ 25¢ 1¢ 10¢ _____

B. 10¢ 25¢ 10¢ 5¢ 10¢ 10¢ 5¢ 1¢ 10¢ 1¢ _____

C. 10¢ 10¢ 1¢ 10¢ 10¢ 10¢ 1¢ 10¢ 1¢ 10¢ _____

D. 5¢ 5¢ 1¢ 25¢ 5¢ 1¢ 1¢ 25¢ _____

Money 2

licorice = 35¢	jelly beans = 29¢
candy corn = 41¢	chocolate stars = 79¢
gumdrops = 53¢	peppermint sticks = 17¢

Write the total spent by each person.

Abby: 1 bag of licorice and 2 bags of jelly beans
_____

Beth: 2 packs of chocolate stars and 4 peppermint sticks _____

Cody: 2 bags of gumdrops and 1 pack of candy corn _____

Dana: 1 of each item _____

Money 3

Kids' Meal Deals

peanut butter and tuna sandwich	$2.75	lima bean cookie	75¢
radish and ketchup on a bun	$1.90	cauliflower soda	$1.15
grape jelly and ham sandwich	$3.25	broccoli ice cream bar	90¢

Write the total for each order.

A. 2 peanut butter and tuna sandwiches and a cauliflower soda _____

B. 1 radish and ketchup on a bun and 3 lima bean cookies _____

C. 8 grape jelly and ham sandwiches and 4 broccoli ice cream bars _____

Money 4

A. Ricardo has 27¢. What is the least number of coins he could have to equal that amount? _____

B. Mario has 19¢. What is the least number of coins he could have to equal that amount?

_____

Money 5

A. Ernie spent $7.17 at the hardware store. How much change did he get from a $10 bill? _____

B. Evie spent $4.71 at the paint store. How much change did she get from a $5 bill?

_____

C. Eddie spent $6.42 for lunch and a tip. How much change did he get from a $20 bill?

_____

Math Warm-ups:
Measurement—Time

Name/Date _____

Measurement—Time 1

A. Joe left home at 7:05 A.M. He arrived at his office 35 minutes later. What time did he arrive? _____

B. Pete rode his motorcycle for 3 hours and 20 minutes. He arrived at 4:10 P.M. What time did he leave? _____

C. Gina needs an hour and a half to get ready for the costume party. The party starts at 8:30 P.M. What time should she start getting ready? _____

D. It takes the make-up department 2 hours and 45 minutes to get the actor who plays the blue alien ready. If he must be ready at 8:20 A.M., what time does he need to start getting his make-up on? _____

Name/Date _____

Measurement—Time 2

	What time is it now?	What time will it be in 20 minutes?
A.	_____	_____
B.	_____	_____
C.	_____	_____

Name/Date _____

Measurement—Time 3

A. If the first of June is on a Monday, on what day of the week will the 11th of June fall? _____

B. Sue left for vacation on May 22 and arrived home 14 days later. What was the date when she returned? _____

C. If the first of August is on a Sunday, how many Sundays will be in the month? _____

Name/Date _____

Measurement—Time 4

A. Ryan needs 14 minutes to shower, 8 minutes to get dressed, 10 minutes to eat breakfast, and 3 minutes to walk to the bus stop. How long does it take Ryan to get ready and get to the bus stop? _____

B. Bea worked in her garden 35 minutes on Monday, 20 minutes on Tuesday, 45 minutes on Wednesday, 15 minutes on Thursday, and 5 minutes on Friday. How many hours did she work in her garden? _____

Name/Date _____

Measurement—Time 5

A. It is 8:40. What time will it be in 2 hours and 20 minutes? _____

B. It is 6:25. What time was it 1 hour and 35 minutes ago? _____

C. It is 9:14. What time will it be in 4 hours and 7 minutes? _____

Math Warm-ups:
Measurement—Length

Name/Date _____

Measurement—Length 1

Write "I" for inches, "F" for feet, "Y" for yards, or "M" for miles to describe the unit of measurement you think would be best for measuring each item.

A. __ A jump rope
B. __ Distance from Miami to Seattle
C. __ A golf club
D. __ Distance from first to second base
E. __ Length of a football field
F. __ A baseball bat

Name/Date _____

Measurement—Length 2

A. 9 feet = _____ yards

B. $\frac{1}{2}$ mile = _____ feet

C. 7 yards = _____ inches

D. 72 inches = _____ yards

E. 5,280 feet = _____ yards

F. 630 feet = _____ yards

Name/Date _____

Measurement—Length 3

A. How much fencing would you need to enclose an area 30 feet wide and 75 feet long?

_____

B. At $15 a foot, how much would it cost to enclose a 10- by 15-yard area?

_____

C. What is the perimeter of a triangle in yards if each side is 13 feet long? _____

D. What is the perimeter of this shape if its base is 8 feet and its height is 3 feet?

_____

Name/Date _____

Measurement—Length 4

A. Kevin ran 440 yards. How many feet did he run? _____
B. Julie used 36 feet of ribbon. How many yards did she use? _____
C. Jamal needed 144 inches of wire. How many feet of wire did he need? _____

D. Rick bought a 90-foot hose. How long was it in yards? _____

Name/Date _____

Measurement—Length 5

Fill in the chart to show the perimeter of each room.

	room	length	width	perimeter
A.	front room	15′	17′	
B.	kitchen	10′	11′	
C.	dining room	12′	14′	
D.	bedroom 1	16′	20′	
E.	bedroom 2	9′	11′	

Math Warm-ups:
Measurement—Volume

Name/Date _____

Measurement—Volume 1

A. Geoff plans to pour a cement slab for a patio. It will be 24 feet by 12 feet by 1 foot deep. How many cubic feet of cement will he need? _____

B. If Geoff makes the slab 20 feet by 12 feet by 1 foot, how many cubic feet less of cement will he need? _____

Name/Date _____

Measurement—Volume 2

A. How many one-inch cubes will fit in a carton 4 inches x 8 inches x 6 inches? _____

B. How many two-inch cubes will fit in a carton the same size? _____

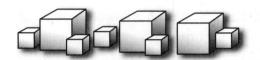

Name/Date _____

Measurement—Volume 3

Max has three containers:

A is 8″ x 8″ x 2″.
B is 9″ x 7″ x 2″.
C is 6″ x 6″ x 4″.

Which container has the greatest volume?

_____

Name/Date _____

Measurement—Volume 4

You have one 3-quart container and two 4-quart containers. Describe how you could measure exactly 2 quarts using only the 3- and 4-quart containers available. Use your own paper for your explanation.

3 QT. 4 QT. 4 QT.

Name/Date _____

Measurement—Volume 5

Label the units of measurement in order from 1 to 5, with 1 being the smallest to 5 being the largest.

A. _____ cup   _____ quart   _____ gallon   _____ ounce   _____ pint

B. _____ 2 cups   _____ 1 quart   _____ 17 ounces   _____ $\frac{1}{2}$ gallon   _____ 5 pints

OUNCES quarts cups gallons pints

Math Warm-ups:
Measurement—Weight

Name/Date _____

Measurement—Weight 1

A. How many one-ounce slices of bread are in a one-pound loaf? _____

B. If eight round crackers weigh one ounce, how many crackers are in a one-pound box? _____

C. Which weighs more: a two-pound can of coffee or a 36-ounce can of coffee? _____

Name/Date _____

Measurement—Weight 2

Circle the items that would weigh about one ounce. Make an X on items that would weigh about one pound.

1 slice of cheese	5 apples	a dozen donuts
2 pats of butter	1 pineapple	8 crackers
2 spoonfuls of peas	a large box of cereal	

Name/Date _____

Measurement—Weight 3

A. A temporary display rack at the hardware store can safely hold up to 200 pounds. Each can of striped paint weighs $9\frac{1}{2}$ pounds. What is the maximum number of cans of paint that can be displayed on this rack? _____

Name/Date _____

Measurement—Weight 4

A. A 12-ounce package of hot dogs contains six hot dogs. How much does each hot dog weigh? _____

B. Which weighs more: a 48-ounce box of potato chips or three pounds of nachos? _____

Name/Date _____

_____

Measurement—Weight 5

Write "O" for ounces, "P" for pounds, or "T" for tons to describe the unit you think would be best for measuring each item.

A. _____ cat

B. _____ elephant

C. _____ semi load of rocks

D. _____ bag of marshmallows

E. _____ refrigerator

F. _____ mouse

G. _____ a great white shark

H. _____ Empire State Building

I. _____ a fruit juice box

J. _____ a bowling ball

Math Warm-ups:
Geometry

Name/Date _____

Geometry 1
Draw shapes that are turned but congruent to the ones shown below.

A.

B.

C.

D.

Name/Date _____

Geometry 2
Draw the next three objects in each pattern.

A. 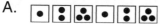 —— —— ——

B.  —— —— ——

C.  —— —— ——

Name/Date _____

Geometry 3
Draw lines of symmetry on each picture.

A.   B.   C.

Name/Date _____

Geometry 4
Connect the dots. Draw a hexagon in box A and an octagon in box B.

A.   B.

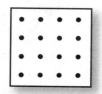 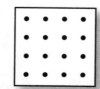

Name/Date _____

Geometry 5
Draw a slide pattern using this shape.

Math Warm-ups:
Geometry

Geometry 6

Draw a repeating pattern using suns, moons, and stars.

Geometry 7

Draw a flip pattern using this shape.

Geometry 8

A. A _____ angle forms a square corner.

B. A _____ is a rectangle with four equal sides.

C. A _____ is a polygon with five sides and five vertices.

D. A _____ is a polygon with three sides and three vertices.

E. A _____ is a three-dimensional figure will all sides being squares the same

shape and size.

Geometry 9

Circle "T" for true or "F" for false. Keep in mind: A polygon is a closed plane figure that has straight lines.

A. T F A rectangle is a polygon.

B. T F A circle is a polygon.

C. T F A cube is a polygon.

D. T F A triangle is not a polygon.

Geometry 10

Draw a turn pattern using this shape.

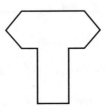

Math Warm-ups:
Geometry

Name/Date _____

Geometry 11
Color or shade to create a pattern.

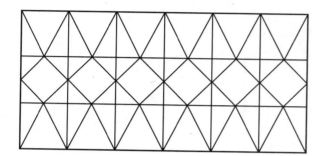

Name/Date _____

Geometry 12
Circle the words that represent three-dimensional objects.

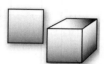

square	circle	sphere	cube
pentagon	pyramid	prism	angle
line	hexagon	hemisphere	cone

Name/Date _____

Geometry 13
In the space below, draw a geometric solid that is not a cube with one face that is square.

Name/Date _____

Geometry 14
Connect the dots. Draw an equilateral triangle in box A. Draw an isosceles triangle in box B.

A.   B.

Name/Date _____

Geometry 15
Write yes or no.

A. Are lines AG and GM parallel? _____

B. Are lines HI and EF parallel? _____

C. Are lines CF and JK perpendicular? _____

D. Are lines DM and IE perpendicular? _____

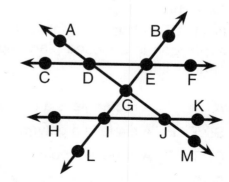

Math Warm-ups:
Probability

Name/Date _____

_____

Probability 1

A. If you grab one of the buttons above without looking, what are the chances of choosing a black button?

_____

B. If you grab one of the buttons above without looking, what are the chances of choosing a black button?

_____

C. What are the chances of choosing a white button?

_____

Name/Date _____

Probability 2
Write "C" for certain, "P" for possible, or "I" for impossible.

A. ____ Saturday will come before Friday this week.

B. ____ You will live to be 100 years old.

C. ____ It will rain tomorrow.

D. ____ You will find a million dollars on your way to school tomorrow.

Name/Date _____

Probability 3

A. What are the chances of spinning an odd number? _____

B. What are the chances of spinning a 4? _____

Name/Date _____

Probability 4

A. If you roll a regular six-sided die, what is the probability of rolling a six? _____

B. Is the probability of rolling five sixes in a row higher, lower, or equal to the probability of rolling five ones in a row? _____

Name/Date _____

Probability 5
Write your full name: _____

A. If you pointed to a letter in your name without looking, what is the probability that it would be an "a"?

_____

B. What is the probability that the letter would be between "t" and "z"? _____

Math Warm-ups:
Brain Teasers

Name/Date _____

Brain Teasers 1

Flora sat in front of Vern.
Jeremy sat between Ming and Vern.
Steve sat to the left of Tom and Flora.
Who sat where? Complete the diagram.

Front			
Back			

Name/Date _____

Brain Teasers 2

Marco has three caps (red, green, and blue) and three t-shirts (pink, orange, and yellow) that he wears to baseball practice. On another sheet of paper, draw a diagram to show the different possible combinations of caps and t-shirts Marco could wear.

Name/Date _____

Brain Teasers 3

Lola arranged her five dragon statues on five shelves, one on each shelf. The dragons were gold, silver, bronze, copper, and crystal. On another sheet of paper, draw a diagram to show all possible arrangements for the five dragons.

Name/Date _____

Brain Teasers 4

Carla planted a fast-growing type of bamboo on June 1. After two weeks, the tallest plant was 24 inches high. During the next two weeks, the weather was perfect, and the bamboo grew 5.6 inches per day. How tall was the plant on June 29?

_____

Name/Date _____

Brain Teasers 5

A circle is two places to the left of a triangle. A square is to the right of a pentagon. The triangle is three places to the right of the rectangle. The square is not on the far left.

Draw the shapes below to show the order in which they are arranged.

Answer Keys

Number Sense and Place Value 1 (p. 2)

	ten thousands	thousands	hundreds	tens	ones
A.	4	3	0	6	7
B.		5	4	3	9
C.	1	0	0	8	0
D.	4	1	0	0	1

Number Sense and Place Value 2 (p. 2)
A. thirty-one thousand, four hundred thirty-eight
B. seventeen thousand ninety-one
C. three thousand seven
D. eight hundred fourteen thousand, seven hundred thirty-seven
E. one million, two hundred fifteen thousand, seventy-six

Number Sense and Place Value 4 (p. 2)
A. 700 + 30 + 9   B. 4,000 + 70 + 8
C. 9,000 + 100 + 90
D. 10,000 + 7,000 + 300 + 70 + 6

Number Sense and Place Value 5 (p. 2)
A. 11,171; 17,117; 17,717; 77,117
B. 27,822; 27,827; 32,287; 83,872
C. 456,456; 456,654; 654,456; 654,654

Number Sense and Place Value 6 (p. 3)
A. < B. > C. < D. < E. > F. =

Number Sense and Place Value 7 (p. 3)
A. 23,332 B. 24,374 C. 91,119 D. 10,111

Number Sense and Place Value 8 (p. 3)
A. 6,640 and 4,066   B. 8,321 and 1,238
C. 9,775 and 5,779   D. 9,820 and 2,089

Number Sense and Place Value 9 (p. 3)
A. 18,428 B. 71,006 C. 15,843 D. 754,108

Number Sense and Place Value 11 (p. 4)
B. 6,510

Number Sense and Place Value 12 (p. 4)
A. 50,914; 41,905; 41,590; 41,095
B. 82,842; 42,282; 24,824; 24,822
C. 453,453; 453,354; 354,453; 354,354

Number Sense and Place Value 13 (p. 4)
A. 88,888 B. 77,373 C. 32,222 D. 91,991

Number Sense and Place Value 14 (p. 4)
A. 10 + 3 = 13 or 3 + 10 = 13
C. 271 > 172 and 172 < 271

Addition 1 (p. 5)
A. 25 B. 37 C. 37 D. 26 E. 26 F. 37

Addition 2 (p. 5)
A. 39   B. 70   C. 151
D. 133   E. 129   F. 104

Addition 3 (p. 5)
A. 84 CDs   B. 30 miles   C. 43 miles

Addition 4 (p. 5)

Wed	Thu	Fri	Sat	Sun	Mon
12	17	22	27	32	37

Addition 5 (p. 5)
Todd surveyed 74 people.

Addition 6 (p. 6)
A. > B. = C. > D. = E. > F. <

Addition 7 (p. 6)
Day 1 38;   Day 2 40;   Day 3 45;
Day 4 53;   Day 5 64;   Day 6 78;
Day 7 95;   Day 8 115;   Day 9 138;
Day 10 164

Addition 8 (p. 6)
A. 40   B. 90   C. 160
D. 110   E. 70   F. 740

Addition 9 (p. 6)
A. 6 + 9 = 15; 9 + 6 = 15; 15 - 6 = 9; 15 - 9 = 6
B. 4 + 7 = 11; 7 + 4 = 11; 11 - 7 = 4; 11 - 4 = 7
C. 8 + 7 = 15; 7 + 8 = 15; 15 - 8 = 7; 15 - 7 = 8
D. 10 + 12 = 22; 12 + 10 = 22; 22 - 10 = 12; 22 - 12 = 10

Addition 10 (p. 6)
A. even   B. even   C. odd   D. odd

Addition 11 (p. 7)
A. 400   B. 500   C. 300
D. 700   E. 600   F. 400

Addition 12 (p. 7)
A. 1,272 B. 2,172 C. 11,172 D. 101,172

Addition 13 (p. 7)
greatest = 549   least = 450

Addition 14 (p. 7)
A. 1789   B. 1998

Addition 15 (p. 7)
A. 161   B. 109   C. 238   D. 54

Addition 16 (p. 8)

A. 23	B. 53	C. 58	D. 68
41	47	51	76
83	65	65	36
102	83	37	44
55	35	86	84

Addition 17 (p. 8)
A. 365 calories   B. 315 calories

Addition 18 (p. 8)
A. 3,000   B. 2,000   C. 32,000 D. 81,000

Addition 19 (p. 8)
greatest = 10,499   least = 9,500

Addition 20 (p. 8)
A. 2109   B. Answer will depend on current year.

Subtraction 1 (p. 9)
A. 13 B. 17 C. 5 D. 36 E. 26 F. 28

Subtraction 2 (p. 9)
A. 12   B. 49

Subtraction 3 (p. 9)
330 pounds

Subtraction 4 (p. 9)
A. even   B. odd   C. odd   D. even

Subtraction 5 (p. 9)
A. 101,072   B. 100,172
C. 91,172   D. 1,172

Subtraction 6 (p. 10)
A. = B. < C. < D. > E. < F. >

Subtraction 7 (p. 10)
A. -9; -12; -15   B. 59; 55; 51
C. 88; 77; 66; 55; 44   D. 408; 307; 206

Subtraction 8 (p. 10)
A. 12 B. 24 C. 11 D. 34 E. 11 F. 9

Subtraction 9 (p. 10)
A. 1743   B. 1911

Subtraction 10 (p. 10)
A. 188   B. 287   C. 7
D. 32   E. 29   F. 93

Subtraction 11 (p. 11)
A. 300   B. 170   C. 540   D. 460

Subtraction 12 (p. 11)
A.

B.

Subtraction 13 (p. 11)
A. $333.71   B. $268.71
C. $189.33   D. $310.67

Subtraction 14 (p. 11)
A. $16.83   B. $32.82

Subtraction 15 (p. 11)
A. F B. F C. T D. F

Subtraction 16 (p. 12)
A. 179 miles   B. 1,336 points

Subtraction 17 (p. 12)
A. 200   B. 700   C. 100   D. 200

Subtraction 18 (p. 12)
A. $2.96   B. $28.89

Subtraction 19 (p. 12)
A. 1821   B. 1898

Subtraction 20 (p. 12)
Teacher check number lines.
A. 8   B. 77   C. 28

Multiplication 1 (p. 13)
A. 24 B. 56 C. 54 D. 35 E. 64 F. 66

Multiplication 2 (p. 13)
A. 32   B. 24   C. 33

Multiplication 3 (p. 13)
A. < B. < C. > D. < E. = F. >

Multiplication 4   (p. 13)
A. $51   B. 108   C. 252

Multiplication 5 (p. 13)
A. 12 B. 21 C. 112   D. 1,125 E. 1,800

Multiplication 6 (p. 14)
A. 105   B. 108   C. 246
D. 560   E. 399   F. 392

Multiplication 7 (p. 14)
A. 224   B. 869   C. 315   D. 112

Multiplication 9 (p. 14)

A. 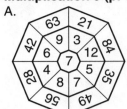   B.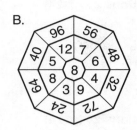

Multiplication 10 (p. 14)

A. $57 B. $292 C. $162 D. $830

Multiplication 11 (p. 15)

A. 1,116 B. $2,790 C. $1,674 D. $4,464

Multiplication 12 (p. 15)

A. 574 B. 2,944 C. 1,944 D. 1,936

Multiplication 13 (p. 15)

A. 42 B. 45 C. 121 D. 52

Multiplication 14 (p. 15)

A. $1.15 B. $15.96 C. $137.84

Multiplication 15 (p. 15)

A. $1.72 B. $2.93 C. $5.20

Division 1 (p. 16)

A. 9 B. 9 C. 8 D. 7 E. 4 F. 6

Division 2 (p. 16)

A. 10 R3 B. 4 R1 C. 4 R0
D. 13 R0 E. 19 R0 F. 13 R3

Division 3 (p. 16)

A. 12 B. 48 C. 69 D. 476

Division 4 (p. 16)

A. 12 B. 51 C. 21

Division 5 (p. 16)

A.	3	B.	7	C.	7	D.	7
	7		6		6		8
	15		9		8		3
	18		12		4		4
	6		4		11		9

Division 6 (p. 17)

A. 7 B. 7 C. 6

Division 7 (p. 17)

A. 88; 88 x 6 = 528 B. 65; 65 x 7 = 455

Division 9 (p. 17)

A. 11 R6 B. 12 R3 C. 3 R3
D. 25 R1 E. 8 R3 F. 10 R4

Division 11 (p. 18)

A. 12 B. 13 C. 12

Division 12 (p. 18)

A. 52 B. 107.5

Division 13 (p. 18)

A. 70

Division 14 (p. 18)

A. 13 B. 12

Division 15 (p. 18)

Friends': 2; 3; 4; 1   Rosa's: 3; 4; 3; 7

Multi-Step Equations 1 (p. 19)

A. 1 B. 14 C. 4

Multi-Step Equations 2 (p. 19)

A. 10 hours   B. $54

Multi-Step Equations 3 (p. 19)

A. $9.44 B. $46.27

Multi-Step Equations 4 (p. 19)

A. = B. > C. < D. >

Multi-Step Equations 5 (p. 19)

A. two for $1.49   B. one for $1.13

Fractions 1 (p. 20)

A. Color 6   B. Color 10

Fractions 2 (p. 20)

A. $\frac{1}{4}$ B. $\frac{2}{3}$ C. $\frac{1}{5}$

D. $\frac{1}{3}$ E. $\frac{3}{5}$ F. $\frac{7}{8}$

Fractions 3 (p. 20)

A. $\frac{1}{2}$; $\frac{5}{8}$; $\frac{7}{10}$; $\frac{3}{4}$; $\frac{7}{8}$

B. $\frac{3}{9}$; $\frac{2}{5}$; $\frac{6}{9}$; $\frac{8}{10}$; $\frac{7}{8}$

C. $\frac{1}{8}$; $\frac{1}{7}$; $\frac{7}{8}$; $\frac{7}{1}$; $\frac{8}{1}$

Fractions 4 (p. 20)

A. $3\frac{4}{11}$ B. $1\frac{3}{4}$ C. 9 D. 46

Fractions 5 (p. 20)

A. $\frac{6}{9} = \frac{2}{3}$ B. $\frac{7}{12}$ C. $\frac{7}{16}$ D. $\frac{3}{10}$

43

Fractions 6 (p. 21)

A. $\frac{10}{25} = \frac{2}{5}$ B. $\frac{4}{16} = \frac{1}{4}$ C. $\frac{16}{26} = \frac{8}{13}$

Fractions 8 (p. 21)

A. $1\frac{1}{4}$ B. $1\frac{1}{7}$ C. $1\frac{2}{9}$ D. $1\frac{1}{2}$

E. $1\frac{1}{6}$ F. $1\frac{5}{6}$

Fractions 10 (p. 21)

A. $\frac{5}{8}$ B. $\frac{2}{9}$ C. $\frac{1}{6}$

D. $\frac{1}{8}$ E. $\frac{3}{10}$ F. $3\frac{1}{3}$

Fractions 11 (p. 22)

A. 18 B. $\frac{1}{3}$ C. 25

Fractions 12 (p. 22)

A. 9 B. 80 C. 24
D. 50 E. 48 F. 36

Fractions 13 (p. 22)

A. 0.3 B. 0.625 C. 0.25 D. 0.125
E. 0.875 F. 0.25 G. 0.375 H. 0.9

Fractions 15 (p. 22)

A. 8 B. 12 remain white

Fractions 16 (p. 23)

A.  B.

Fractions 17 (p. 23)

A. 50% B. 75% C. 70%
D. 65% E. 4% F. 25%

Fractions 18 (p. 23)

A. $\frac{2}{9}$ B. $\frac{3}{28}$ C. $\frac{5}{36}$

D. $\frac{1}{48}$ E. $\frac{1}{72}$ F. $\frac{15}{56}$

Fractions 19 (p. 23)

A. 37¢ B. $1.26

Fractions 20 (p. 23)

A. $\frac{1}{3}$ B. $1\frac{1}{2}$ C. 2 D. $\frac{1}{56}$

Fractions 23 (p. 24)

A. $\frac{1}{16}$; $\frac{1}{32}$; $\frac{1}{64}$

B. $\frac{8}{16}$; $\frac{10}{16}$; $\frac{12}{16}$

C. $\frac{5}{12}$; $\frac{3}{12}$; $\frac{1}{12}$

Fractions 24 (p. 24)

A. $\frac{5}{11}$ B. $\frac{2}{11}$ C. $\frac{9}{11}$

Math Terms to Know 1 (p. 25)
A. difference B. denominator C. numerator
D. dividend E. divisor

Math Terms to Know 2 (p. 25)
A. e B. c C. f D. b E. d F. a

Math Terms to Know 3 (p. 25)
A. T B. F C. T D. F E. T

Math Terms to Know 4 (p. 25)
A. 2 B. 32 C. 12 D. 6 E. 8

Math Terms to Know 5 (p. 25)

A. $3\frac{1}{2}$ B. $\frac{1}{2}$ and $\frac{4}{8}$ C. 11
D. 1,000 grams E. $7 \div 5$

Algebra 1 (p. 26)
A. 18 B. 24 C. 8 D. 24 E. 6 F. 4

Algebra 2 (p. 26)
A. 25 B. 4 C. 33 D. 9 E. 4
F. (1)9 or (2)6 or (3)3 or (4)0

Algebra 3 (p. 26)
A. 25 B. 4 C. 33 D. 9 E. 4 F. 3

Algebra 4 (p. 26)
A. $71 - x = 38$; $x = 33$ B. $72 \div x = 8$; $x = 9$

Algebra 5 (p. 26)
A. $42 - x = 17$; $x = 25$ B. $24 \div x = 6$; $x = 4$
   or $17 + x = 4$; $x = 25$ or $6 \cdot x = 24$; $x = 4$

Tables and Graphs 2 (p. 27)

A. 100 B. 11% C. $\frac{4}{25}$ D. 0.13

Tables and Graphs 4 (p. 27)
A. lynx B. leopard
C. tiger, cheetah, leopard, cougar, lion, lynx

Decimals 1 (p. 28)
A. 0.08   B. 11.12   C. 0.81
D. 14.6   E. 0.21   F. 7.07

Decimals 2 (p. 28)
A. $4.56   B. $0.72   C. $15.48   D. $9.02

Decimals 3 (p. 28)
A. $\frac{39}{50}$ B. $\frac{5}{8}$ C. $\frac{99}{100}$ D. $\frac{13}{50}$

Decimals 4 (p. 28)
A. 8.6   B. 14.3   C. 12.0
D. 1.9   E. 8.9   F. 1.6

Decimals 5 (p. 28)
A. 20.2°   B. 24.7°   C. 3.8°   D. 10.5°

Decimals 6 (p. 29)
A. 18.13   B. 33.06   C. 34.31

Decimals 7 (p. 29)
A. 25.9 miles   B. 285 pies

Decimals 8 (p. 29)
A. 54.9   B. 30

Decimals 9 (p. 29)
A. 0.37   B. 0.42   C. 0.914
D. 0.037   E. 0.265   F. 0.062

Decimals 10 (p. 29)
A. Shade in 75 squares   B. Shade in 33 squares
C. Shade in 87 squares   D. Shade in 4 squares

Decimals 11 (p. 30)
A. $3\frac{7}{10}$ B. $4\frac{31}{50}$ C. $11\frac{1}{10}$ D. $9\frac{13}{20}$

Decimals 12 (p. 30)
A. 2,083.2   B. $10.46

Decimals 13 (p. 30)
A. 3.6   B. 3.6   C. 8.59   D. 17.52

Decimals 14 (p. 30)
A. $36.75   B. $49.35

Decimals 15 (p. 30)

Fraction	Percent	Decimal
A. $\frac{7}{8}$	87.5%	0.875
B. $\frac{3}{4}$	75%	0.75
C. $\frac{29}{40}$	72.5%	0.725

Fraction	Percent	Decimal
D. $1\frac{7}{20}$	135%	1.35
E. $\frac{5}{8}$	62.5%	0.625
F. $\frac{4}{6}$	66.7%	0.667

Money 1 (p. 31)
A. $1.18   B. 87¢   C. 73¢   D. 68¢

Money 2 (p. 31)
A. 93¢   B. $2.26   C. $1.47   D. $2.54

Money 3 (p. 31)
A. $6.65   B. $4.15   C. $29.60

Money 4 (p. 31)
A. 3 (1 quarter and 2 pennies)
B. 6 (1 dime, 1 nickel, and 4 pennies)

Money 5 (p. 31)
A. $2.83   B. 29¢   C. $13.58

Measurement—Time 1 (p. 32)
A. 7:40 A.M.   B. 12:50 P.M.
C. 7:00 P.M.   D. 5:35 A.M.

Measurement—Time 2 (p. 32)
A. 7:30   7:50   B. 2:45   3:05
C. 10:05   10:25

Measurement—Time 3 (p. 32)
A. Thursday   B. June 5   C. 5

Measurement—Time 4 (p. 32)
A. 35 minutes   B. 2 hours

Measurement—Time 5 (p. 32)
A. 11:00   B. 4:50   C. 1:21

Measurement—Length 1 (p. 33)
A. I or F   B. M   C. I or F
D. F or Y   E. Y   F. I or F

Measurement—Length 2 (p. 33)
A. 3   B. 2,640   C. 252
D. 2   E. 1,760   F. 210

Measurement—Length 3 (p. 33)
A. 210 feet   B. $2,250
C. 13 yards   D. 22 feet

Measurement—Length 4 (p. 33)
A. 1,320 feet   B. 12 yards
C. 12 feet   D. 30 yards

Measurement—Length 5 (p. 33)
A. 64′ B. 42′ C. 52′
D. 72′ E. 40′

Measurement—Volume 1 (p. 34)
A. 288 cubic feet B. 48 cubic feet less

Measurement—Volume 2 (p. 34)
A. 192 B. 24

Measurement—Volume 3 (p. 34)
C has the most volume: 144 cubic inches.

Measurement—Volume 4 (p. 34)
Fill the 4-quart container and pour it into the 3-quart container, leaving 1 quart. Put that aside. Empty the 3-quart container. Fill the other 4-quart container and pour it into the 3-quart container. Add the 1 quart left to the 1 quart you set aside for a total of 2 quarts.

Measurement—Volume 5 (p. 34)
A. ounce; cup; pint; quart; gallon

B. 2 cups; 17 ounces; 1 quart; $\frac{1}{2}$ gallon; 5 pints

Measurement—Weight 1 (p. 35)
A. 16 B. 128 C. 36-ounce can of coffee

Measurement—Weight 2 (p. 35)
About 1 ounce: cheese, butter, crackers, peas
About 1 pound: apples, donuts, pineapple, cereal

Measurement—Weight 3 (p. 35)
A. 21

Measurement—Weight 4 (p. 35)
A. 2 ounces B. They weigh the same.

Measurement—Weight 5 (p. 35)
A. P B. P or T C. T D. O E. P
F. O G. P H. T I. O J. P

Geometry 2 (p. 36)
A.
B.
C.

Geometry 3 (p. 36)
A. B. C.

Geometry 8 (p. 37)
A. right B. square C. pentagon
D. triangle E. cube

Geometry 9 (p. 37)
A. T B. F C. F D. F

Geometry 12 (p. 38)
Circle the sphere, cube, pyramid, prism, hemisphere, and cone.

Geometry 13 (p. 38)

Geometry 15 (p. 38)
A. no B. yes C. no D. yes

Probability 1 (p. 39)
A. 7 in 10 B. 2 in 8 or 1 in 4 C. 3 in 8

Probability 2 (p. 39)
A. I B. P
C. P (Depends on time of year and area where you live.)
D. P (Hey, it could happen!)

Probability 3 (p. 39)
A. 2 in 6 or 1 in 3 B. 3 in 6 or 1 in 2

Probability 4 (p. 39)
A. 1 in 6 B. equal to

Brain Teasers 1 (p. 40)
Front: Steve/Tom/Flora
Back: Ming/Jeremy/Vern

Brain Teasers 2 (p. 40)
The nine possible combinations are:
R & P B & P G & P
R & O B & O G & O
R & Y B & Y G & Y

Brain Teasers 3 (p. 40)
There are 20 possible combinations.

Brain Teasers 4 (p. 40)
102.4 inches [It was 24 inches tall on June 15 (2 weeks after June 1). It grew 5.6 inches per day for 2 more weeks (14 x 5.6 = 78.4), plus the original 24 inches = 102.4 inches.]

Brain Teasers 5 (p. 40)
rectangle, circle, pentagon, triangle, square